Powell's  Peaceful Leader: Martin Luther

$33.99 / 5.98    PC

Children's                    117463

# PEACEFUL LEADER
# MARTIN LUTHER KING JR.

By BRUCE BEDNARCHUK

Illustrated by MARCIN PIWOWARSKI

CANTATA LEARNING

MANKATO, MINNESOTA

**CANTATA LEARNING**
MANKATO, MINNESOTA

Published by Cantata Learning
1710 Roe Crest Drive
North Mankato, MN 56003
www.cantatalearning.com

Copyright © 2015 Cantata Learning

All rights reserved. No part of this publication may be reproduced
in any form without written permission from the publisher.

Library of Congress Control Number: 2014938334
ISBN: 978-1-63290-086-9

*Peaceful Leader: Martin Luther King Jr.* by Bruce Bednarchuck
Illustrated by Marcin Piwowarski

Book design by Tim Palin Creative
Music produced by Wes Schuck
Audio recorded, mixed, and mastered at Two Fish Studios, Mankato, MN

Printed in the United States of America.

Martin Luther King, Jr.
(1929–1968)

Martin Luther King, Jr. was born into the world at a time when people were treated differently because of their skin color. He believed everyone should be treated equally. Martin Luther King, Jr. devoted his life to peaceful protests and working towards change in his country. He was a leader to many and changed America for the better.

Way down in Georgia in 1929,
Martin Luther King, Jr. was born.

When he was a young man, he became a **preacher**,
who would later bring hope to a nation racially torn.

He was awarded the Nobel Peace Prize.

He said, "I have a dream," and the world could not deny.

With peaceful **protests**, he helped shape **civil rights**, so that people of all colors could unite.

Martin Luther King, Jr. worked so hard
to change all **segregation** laws.

He led a **boycott**, and they marched in Washington.

And his "I Have a Dream" speech came from
a most righteous cause.

He was awarded the Nobel Peace Prize.

He said, "I have a dream," and the world could not deny.

With peaceful protests, he helped shape civil rights,

so that people of all colors could unite.

Yes, he had a dream, and that dream lives today.

We still have such a long way to go
to make sure we love our neighbors and our hearts never stray
from the goodness and the truths we have come to know.

He was awarded the Nobel Peace Prize.

He said, "I have a dream," and the world could not deny.

With peaceful protests, he helped shape civil rights,
so that people of all colors could unite.

In 1968, Dr. King died. But his legacy of hope remains strong. That's why we celebrate every January, so we can continue to learn about what is right and wrong.

He was awarded the Nobel Peace Prize.

He said, "I have a dream," and the world could not deny.

With peaceful protests, he helped shape civil rights,
so that people of all colors could unite.

So that people of all colors could unite.

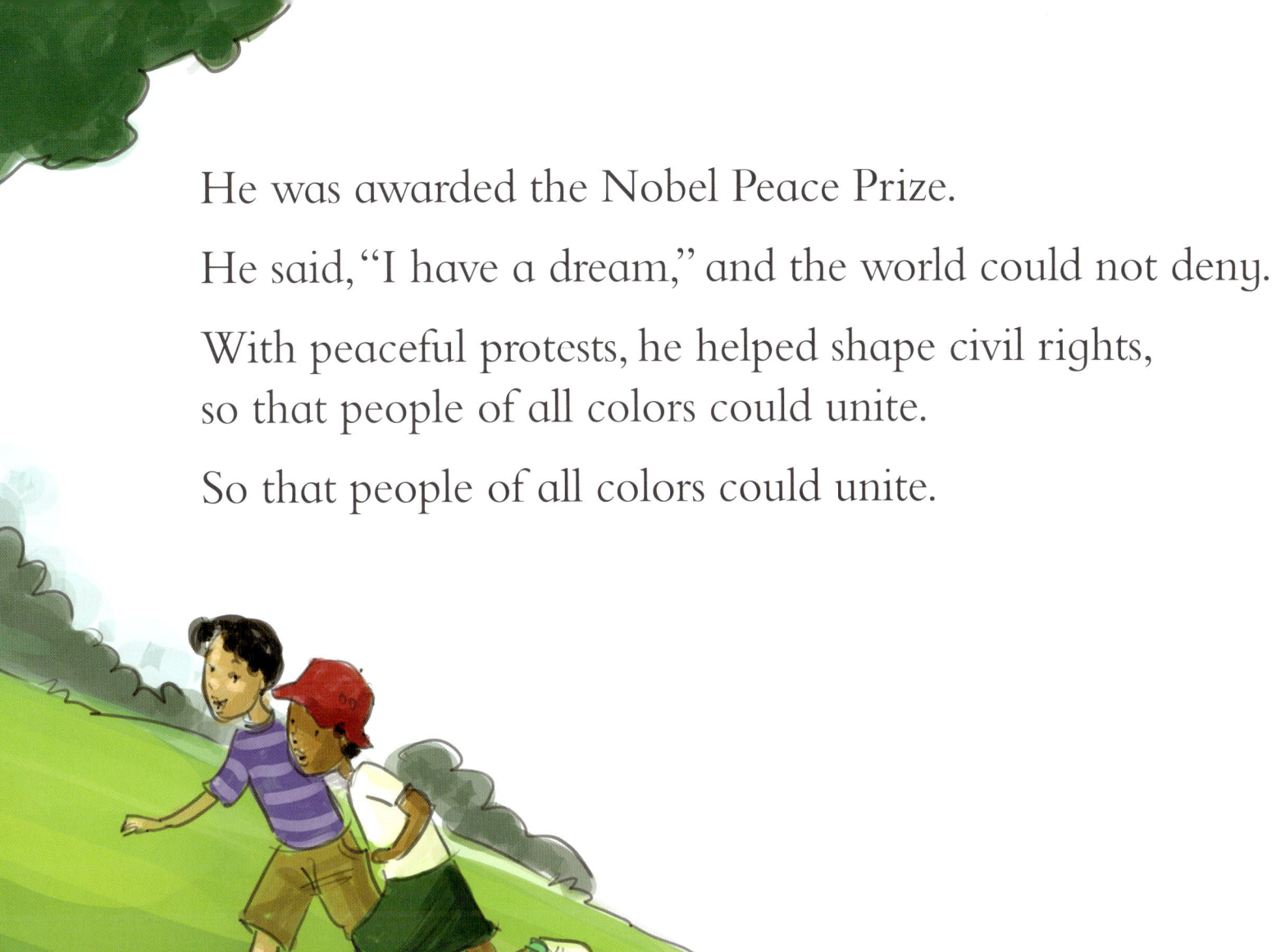

# GLOSSARY

**boycott**—to refuse to take part in something as a way of making a protest

**civil rights**—freedoms that every person should have

**preacher**—a person who gives religious speeches

**protest**—to object to something strongly and publicly

**segregation**—separating people because of their skin color

# Peaceful Leader: Martin Luther King Jr.

Bruce Bednarchuk
Contemporary

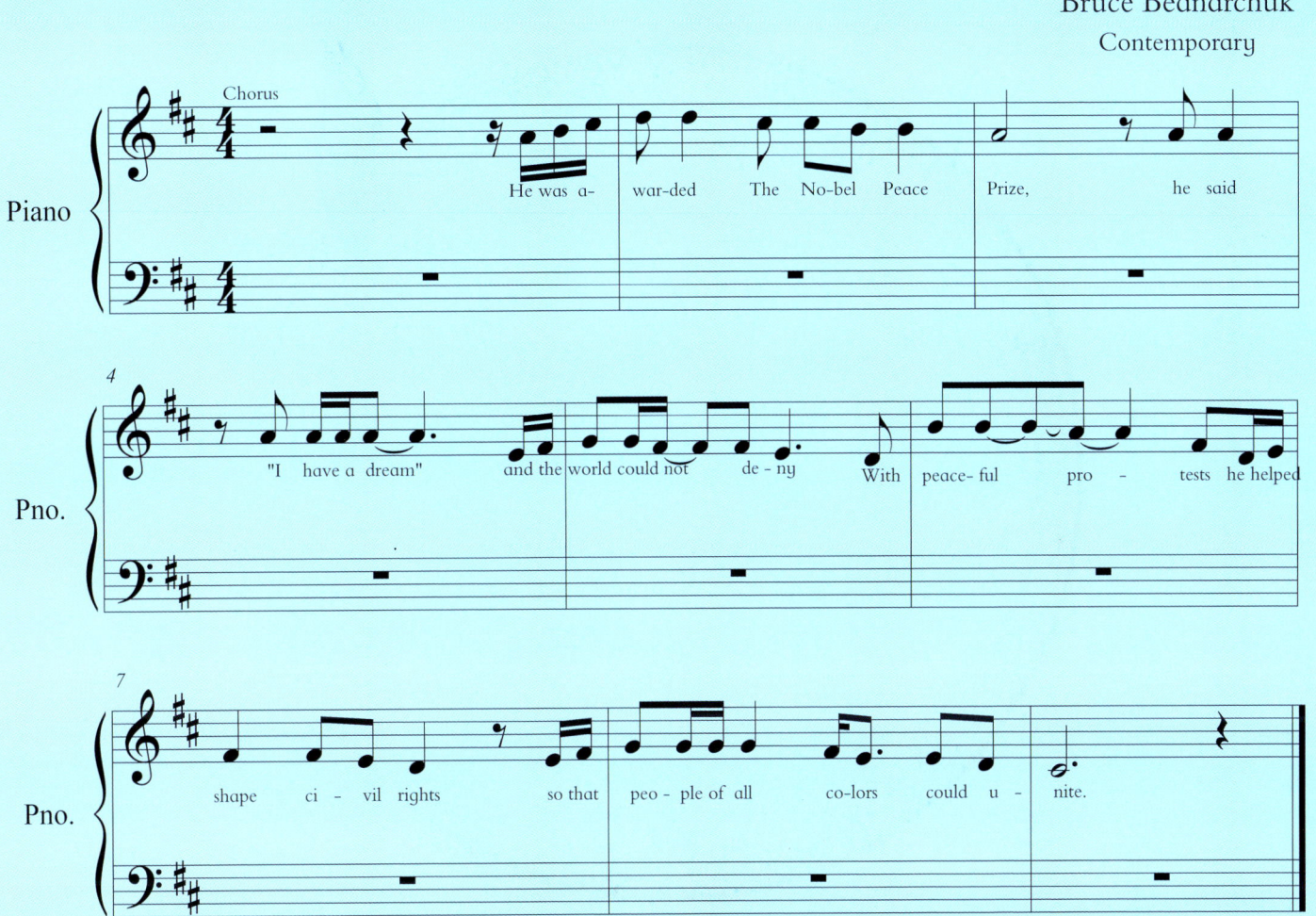

Online music access and CDs available at **www.cantatalearning.com**

# ACTIVITY

1. Segregation means to keep people apart because of their skin color. What did Martin Luther King, Jr. do to help end segregation?

2. Have you ever felt like you needed to stand up for someone? Tell a friend, draw a picture, or write a story about your experience.

3. When should people have equal rights? Sometimes? Always? Explain your answer.

# TO LEARN MORE

Bauer, Marion Dane. *Martin Luther King, Jr.* New York: Scholastic, 2009.

Cella, Clara. *Martin Luther King, Jr. Day.* Mankato, MN: Capstone Press, 2013.

Flynn, Riley. *Martin Luther King Jr.* Mankato, MN: Capstone Press, 2014.

Jazynka, Kitson. *Martin Luther King, Jr.* New York: National Geographic Children's Books, 2012.